Wild

Written by
Jack Ashby

Illustrated by
Sara Boccaccini Meadows

MAGIC CAT 🐱 PUBLISHING

NEW YORK

I am very lucky—I work in a natural history museum, where millions of animal specimens from across the world have been brought together into one place. Museums allow us to spot similarities and differences between species, which can tell us about how they are related and how they are perfectly shaped to live their lives.

One thing that fascinates me is when animals look incredibly similar but are not closely related. I find it completely mind-blowing, for example, that a certain predator in Australia looks exactly like a striped wolf, even though it's not even a member of the wolf family. It's called a thylacine, and it's a marsupial, related to koalas and kangaroos.

Thylacines and wolves look the same because they do the same things in their habitats, and so they evolved the same adaptations, separately, on opposite sides of the world. This book explores other examples of animals that have the same adaptation, even though they belong to different groups.

Each chapter looks at a different adaptation and shows how similarities can appear again and again in different groups of vertebrates (animals with backbones: birds, mammals, fish, amphibians, and reptiles). When different animals evolve the same adaptation to do the same job, this pattern is called convergent evolution.

I hope that this book encourages you to look closely at nature, to spot other examples and patterns where species that are different in many ways also have something important in common.

—J.A.

CONTENTS

the HERO OF BEING PRICKLY

the EASTERN LONG-BEAKED ECHIDNA

Animals can have many different coverings, from hair to scales, from feathers to smooth skin. Some have modified their covering to form defensive spines, and long-beaked echidnas are among the very largest prickly beasts.

EASTERN LONG-BEAKED ECHIDNA
ZAGLOSSUS BARTONI

While crunchy things can be nice to eat, having spiky things in your mouth is a horrible, painful feeling. Many animals (and plants) have evolved prickles as an excellent defense against being eaten by predators.

WHERE IN THE WILD?
Eastern long-beaked echidnas live in the mountains and grasslands of New Guinea.

They are critically endangered and can be hard to track down. Their cousins, short-beaked echidnas, are much easier to find. They are the most widespread mammals in Australia, where they can be found day and night, in every habitat on land, hunting for ants.

Echidnas and their platypus relatives are the only mammals that **lay eggs**. After hatching, baby echidnas are called **"puggles"** and are protected in their mother's pouch.

Eastern long-beaked echidnas mainly eat earthworms. They have **spines on their tongues** for added grip as they pull the wriggly worms into their mouths.

snouts that detect electricity

Echidnas can find their prey by detecting electricity with their **toothless snouts**. All animals' muscles produce electrical signals, which echidnas can sense in wet soil.

THE TROUBLE WITH SPINES
Prickly hedgehogs are famously riddled with fleas. Spiny animals can struggle to clean themselves, as their spines work just as well against their own hands and faces as they do against predators. Echidnas have solved this problem: Their hindfeet have long claws, point backward, and are highly flexible, allowing them to reach across their entire bodies and safely scratch between their spines.

ALL ABOUT PRICKLES

Every animal needs protection against predators. This has resulted in many defensive adaptations, including camouflage, armor, poison, venom, tasting bad, or simply growing to be massive. Spines have also evolved in lots of animal groups by modifying hairs, scales, skin . . . and even bone.

Erinaceus europaeus

WESTERN EUROPEAN HEDGEHOG
Hedgehogs have a sheet of **muscle** under their skin that rolls them into a spiky ball.

Echinops telfairi

LESSER HEDGEHOG TENREC
Although these Madagascan mammals look strikingly like hedgehogs, they are actually more closely related to **elephants**.

SHARP-RIBBED NEWT
If attacked, these soft-skinned amphibians create prickles by pushing their **spiky ribs** through their own skin, picking up venom on the way.

Pleurodeles waltl

PRICKLES AROUND THE WORLD

The thorny devil's scientific name is **Moloch**, which is also the name of a feared ancient horned Canaanite deity in the Bible.

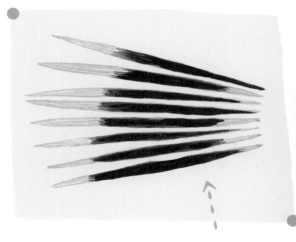

In Anishinaabe accounts, porcupines from around the Great Lakes of North America got their **quills** when hawthorn thorns were stuck in one's back with clay as protection against the bear and wolf.

SPOT-FIN PORCUPINEFISH

When threatened, porcupinefish **inflate** their body with air or water, making their spines (which are modified scales) stick outward.

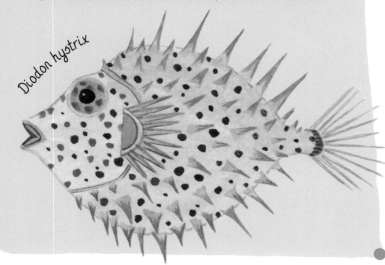

Diodon hystrix

THORNY DEVIL

Scales on these Australian lizards resemble **thorns** and act as both camouflage and defense. They can also change color to match their background.

Moloch horridus

DETACHABLE QUILLS

The **North American porcupine** can have tens of thousands of quills, which are extremely sharp and can detach from the porcupine to remain stuck in their predator. Each spine is covered in microscopic backward-facing barbs that grip the attacker's skin, making them difficult and painful to remove.

Erethizon dorsatum

In several First Nations Australian accounts, echidna spines originate from when their ancestor was attacked and its back was **pierced** by many spears.

Warriors on the Pacific island of Kiribati made intimidating helmets from inflated **porcupinefish** skins, known as "te barantauti," as part of their armor.

the HERO OF ENDLESS TEETH

the GREAT WHITE SHARK

Damaged teeth cause all sorts of problems, which is why—unlike humans—most animals with teeth use different tactics to continually replace theirs. Some sharks can go through tens of thousands of teeth throughout their lives.

GREAT WHITE SHARK
Carcharodon carcharias

If all of an animal's teeth fell out, it would not be able to eat. When sharks lose a tooth—which can be every few weeks—another one comes in from behind to replace it. Imagine never having a toothache!

WHERE IN THE WILD?
Great white sharks are the largest living predatory fish.

They are found almost anywhere that water doesn't get too cold. When they start feeling a chill, they will migrate to warmer waters. The biggest populations live around the coasts of the USA, Japan, Australia, New Zealand, South America, Africa, and the Mediterranean.

A great white's jaws have about 50 teeth in use at once, but behind these are more **rows of teeth**, waiting for the ones in front to fall out. They never stop growing new teeth.

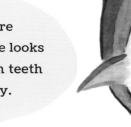

many rows of teeth

A great white's teeth are **triangular**, and each side looks like a little saw. The bottom teeth are narrow to grip prey.

THE TROUBLE WITH OUR TEETH
Unlike sharks, almost all mammals (including humans) only have one set of baby teeth and one set of adult teeth. This is because our teeth are too complex to replace: the lumps and bumps on our top and bottom teeth must fit together perfectly so they can slice, grind, and crush all at once. If we lose an adult tooth, it's gone forever.

If a great white bites into a big animal, like a seal, whale, or other shark, they shake their head from side to side to **saw off** a chunk of meat.

ALL ABOUT ENDLESS TEETH

Birds and turtles don't have teeth, but other vertebrates have evolved different ways to replace lost teeth. Some mammals have changed the way their teeth grow to make them last longer. Our own teeth are unusual in being so firmly attached to our jawbones.

Vombatus ursinus

COMMON WOMBAT

These marsupials' teeth never stop **growing**. As the tough plants they eat wear down the surface, the tooth just grows a bit longer.

Crocodylus niloticus

NILE CROCODILE

In crocodiles, **replacement teeth** grow inside the tooth they're replacing. When one falls out, another is already there beneath it.

Bitis gabonica

GABOON VIPER

Over time, the inside of a snake's tooth eats itself away, so older teeth become weak and **fall out**, making space for new ones.

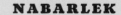

Loxodonta africana

AFRICAN BUSH ELEPHANT

In its adult set of teeth, an elephant has **six** chewing teeth on each side of its jaw. The teeth appear one at a time so the set lasts longer.

NABARLEK

These tiny rock-wallabies are extremely unusual among mammals: They have an **unlimited** number of teeth. They replace their teeth endlessly, like sharks.

Petrogale concinna

METAL BITE

A mammal's front teeth, called incisors, are mainly used for cutting. Rodents, including mice, squirrels, beavers, and the **brown rat** pictured here, have incisors that never stop growing and can sharpen themselves. The front layer of a rodent's incisors can contain iron and is harder than the back layer. Every time the animal bites down, the back wears more quickly than the front, creating a super-sharp blade.

Rattus norvegicus

ENDLESS TEETH AROUND THE WORLD

Traditional **Hawaiian** weapons called "leiomano" include tiny knives and large-bladed clubs made by attaching sharks' teeth to wooden handles.

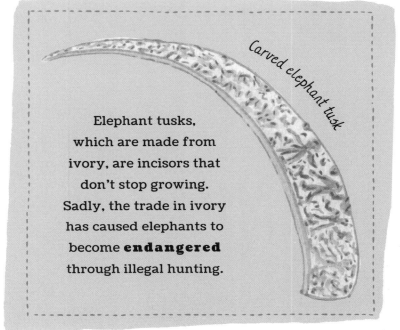

Elephant tusks, which are made from ivory, are incisors that don't stop growing. Sadly, the trade in ivory has caused elephants to become **endangered** through illegal hunting.

Carved elephant tusk

Because they are so sharp, rodent incisors have been used as **cutting tools** throughout the world. For example, Iroquoian people in Canada used beaver teeth to carve wood.

beaver-tooth carving tool

Historically, in the **Philippines**, warrior chiefs wore necklaces made of crocodile teeth as symbols of their power.

the HERO OF GLIDING

the GREATER GLIDER

Flapping flight has only evolved three times in vertebrates (in birds, bats, and pterosaurs—flying reptiles from the time of dinosaurs). However, gliding, or using body parts as parachutes, has evolved many times.

Flying by beating one's wings takes a lot of energy, but gliding through the air with a single jump is much easier. Greater gliders are tree-climbing mammals that can leap vast distances from tree to tree to escape predators or find food.

WHERE IN THE WILD?

Greater gliders are a kind of possum found in eastern Australia.

They prefer mountain forests where there are plenty of big eucalyptus trees; they live in hollows in the trunks, which only appear as trees get older. We must protect their populations by preventing bushfires and stopping trees from being cut down.

Greater gliders have a **parachute of skin** between their arms and legs that ends at their elbows. To glide, they fold their hands under their chins, elbows out.

A greater glider is the size of a cat, but weighs much less. They can glide more than **300 feet** (100 m) between trees without a single wingbeat.

a parachute between their arms and legs

POSSUMS WITH POSSIBILITIES

Possums are tree-dwelling marsupials (the group that also contains kangaroos and koalas). Just like greater gliders, other kinds of possums have evolved gliding adaptations: Sugar gliders become flat squares when they glide— their skin-parachutes connect their ankles to their fingertips. And tiny, feather-tailed gliders use a fringe of long hairs along each side of their tail.

extra-long tail for steering

Their massive, **fluffy tails** are longer than their bodies and keep greater gliders stable, allowing them to steer in midair. They can even turn corners while gliding.

ALL ABOUT GLIDING

The most common gliding adaptations involve stretching a sheet of skin between different body parts, but some groups do things differently: by flattening their whole bodies out. All gliders have evolved to catch air as they fall, forming a parachute that slows their descent and allows them to glide forward great distances.

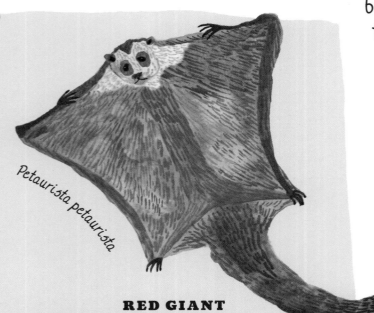

Petaurista petaurista

RED GIANT FLYING SQUIRREL

Flying squirrels' **parachutes** stretch between their wrists and ankles. They have an extra structure in their wrists to help control its shape.

ABAH RIVER FLYING FROG

Flying frogs have extra-long **webbed toes**, which act as four parachutes when they leap.

Rhacophorus nigropalmatus

ADAPTATION

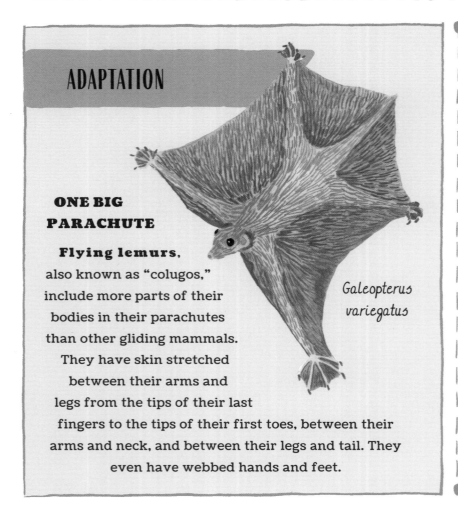

ONE BIG PARACHUTE

Flying lemurs, also known as "colugos," include more parts of their bodies in their parachutes than other gliding mammals. They have skin stretched between their arms and legs from the tips of their last fingers to the tips of their first toes, between their arms and neck, and between their legs and tail. They even have webbed hands and feet.

Galeopterus variegatus

GLIDING AROUND THE WORLD

A story from Australia's Daly River region tells that storms in the Wet Season are caused by **sugar gliders** moving clouds across the sky.

Petaurus breviceps

COMMON FLYING DRAGON

These Asian lizards have extremely long **ribs** that they can fold out to form their gliding "wing."

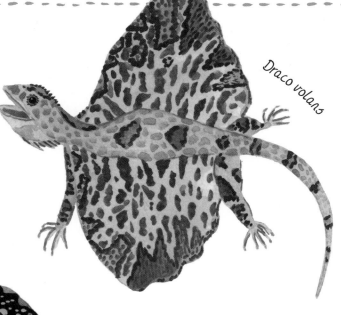

Draco volans

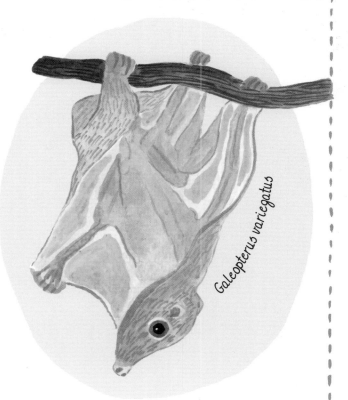

Galeopterus variegatus

Chrysopelea paradisi

PARADISE FLYING SNAKE

Flying snakes suck in their bellies and push their ribs out sideways to **flatten** themselves, then move their bodies in a wave to glide through their air.

SUNDA FLYING LEMUR

Flying lemurs aren't truly lemurs and can't truly fly, but they can **glide**. They aren't members of the primate group, but are closely related.

風狸

Chinese mythical gliding creatures called **"fengli"** may be based on flying lemurs. Fengli are said to carry a wand that stops other animals from running or flying.

One species of flying squirrel, the Siberian flying squirrel, lives in far northeast Europe. In Finnish legend, their bodies contain a magical force known as **"väki."**

Pteromys volans

In Japanese folklore, a dangerous creature called a **"nobusuma"** looks like a flying squirrel and can drain the life from their victims.

the HERO OF VENOM

the FIERCE SNAKE

When size or strength isn't on your side, injecting venom into your prey or your enemies can be the ultimate deadly tactic for both attack and defense.

FIERCE SNAKE
OXYURANUS MICROLEPIDOTUS

Producing venom to kill or weaken other animals is a powerful adaptation; it can stop them from being able to attack or fight back. Fierce snakes have the strongest venom of any reptile, which they mainly use for hunting mammals.

WHERE IN THE WILD?

Also called inland taipan, fierce snakes are found in the deserts of eastern Central Australia, where it gets very hot in the summer, but is much cooler in winter.

To help them survive, these snakes change color with the seasons; dark colors take in more heat, and fierce snakes are darker in winter.

These snakes grow incredibly quickly, getting more than 2 inches (5 cm) longer every month! At full size, they can reach more than **6 feet** (1.8 m).

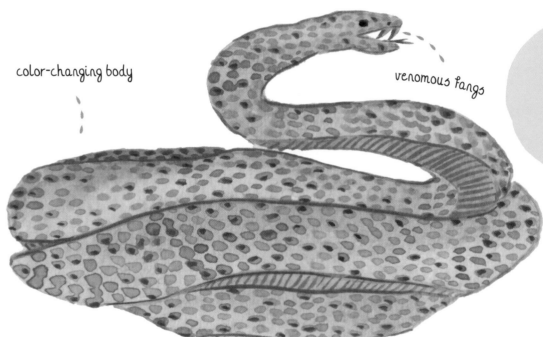

color-changing body

venomous fangs

A single bite from a fierce snake can inject enough venom to kill well over **100,000 mice**— far deadlier than any other species.

Being big and having **powerful venom** is helpful for hunting larger rodents like long-haired rats, which have strong, sharp teeth for defense.

VENOMOUS OR DANGEROUS?

Being the most venomous snake doesn't make our hero the most dangerous. Fierce snakes are not fierce at all, but are a shy and calm species. But don't take any chances—although they prefer to hide away when threatened, they will use their venom if they can't easily escape.

VENOM

15

VENOM

ALL ABOUT VENOM

Venom and poison are not the same thing. Poison is eaten. Venom is injected through the skin by using something sharp like teeth, spines, or stings. Both cause pain or stop the victim's body working properly. There are no known venomous birds, but many other animals have adaptations for injecting venom.

Nycticebus coucang

GREATER SLOW LORIS

These Asian primates produce some venom in their mouths and another **toxin** on their arms, which they lick before biting their rivals.

GILA MONSTER

There aren't many venomous lizards, but this North American species has **grooved** teeth to inject its venom, which is mainly used for defense.

Heloderma suspectum

Nyctimantis brunoi

BRUNO'S CASQUE-HEADED FROG

Many frogs are poisonous if predators eat them, but this Brazilian species can attack: It has tiny spines on its **head** to inject venom.

Ornithorhynchus anatinus

DEVIL FIREFISH

Also called "lionfish," this colorful species defends itself from predators using venom from spines in its **fins**.

Pterois miles

PLATYPUS

Only male platypuses are venomous. They have thick, horny venom spurs by their **ankles**, which they use for fighting each other over mates.

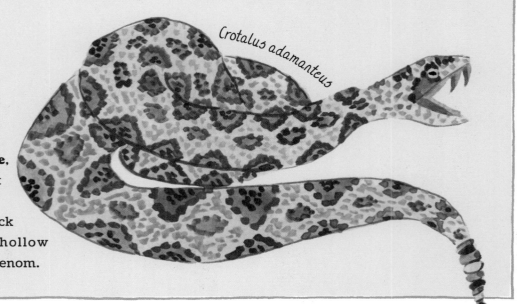

Crotalus adamanteus

FOLDING FANGS

Snake fangs are amazing. Many species, like the **eastern diamondback rattlesnake**, have front teeth that would be too long to fit in their mouths, but they fold flat along the tongue when their mouths are closed and flick out forward when they open. Their fangs are hollow tubes—like doctors' needles—to inject venom.

VENOM AROUND THE WORLD

In an Indigenous Australian creation story, the platypus is the child of a duck named **Gaygar** and a spear-carrying water rat named **Bigoon**. Platypuses' venomous spurs represent Bigoon's sharp spear.

Venomous Indian cobras are often linked with **Hindu** gods and are shown wrapped around Ganesha's waist or Shiva's neck, or supporting Vishnu as he rests.

Some people in Indonesia believe that the venomous slow lorises are **bad luck** and must not be disturbed.

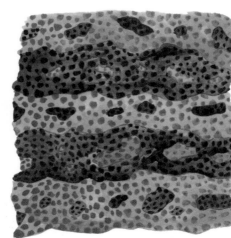

An Apache belief states that a Gila monster's **breath** is deadly, while Yaqui people believe its **skin** has healing powers.

the HERO OF WARNING COLORS

the GOLDEN POISON FROG

If an animal is toxic, a dangerous fighter, or tastes terrible, predators will want to know before attacking. Bright colors can be a warning to other animals.

GOLDEN POISON FROG
PHYLLOBATES TERRIBILIS

Many animals try to hide from predators and enemies, but have you ever wondered why some species have colors or patterns that make them stand out? This can be a tactic to let other animals know that it might not be a good idea to attack.

WHERE IN THE WILD?

Golden poison frogs are an endangered species found on the Amazon rainforest floor in Colombia.

Their bright yellow-golden color makes them easy to spot on the dark brown dead leaves they live among. This is a warning sign to predators: "Don't eat me: I'm the most poisonous frog in the world."

bright-yellow skin

The skin of a golden poison frog oozes a deadly poison that, if eaten, stops predators' **muscles** from working, including their hearts.

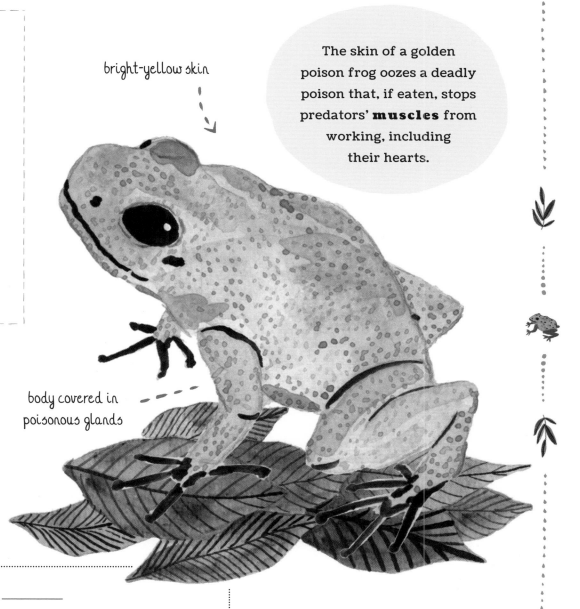

body covered in poisonous glands

They are a species of **poison dart frog**. Other poison dart frogs have blue, orange, and green warning colors, or black and yellow like wasps.

FAKING IT

Most animals with warning colors have some form of defense that can make predators decide not to attack. However, many harmless animals have evolved similar colors. This is a trick to make possible attackers think they are dangerous too. For example, milk snakes—which are harmless—have similar colors to venomous coral snakes.

Females lay **eggs** on land. When they hatch, male frogs put the tadpoles on their backs and carry them to water, where the tadpoles grow into froglets.

ALL ABOUT WARNING COLORS

The best way of defending yourself is to stop an attack before it happens because even if you're the most poisonous animal on earth, you will probably get hurt if a predator bites you. Many animals with strong defenses have evolved warning colors to warn attackers.

STRIPED SKUNK

Defense isn't all about poison and venom. A skunk's strong black-and-white pattern warns predators that they can spray a **disgusting scent** from their bottoms.

Mephitis mephitis

HOODED PITOHUI

Living in the forests of New Guinea, this orange-and-black bird has **poisons** in its skin and feathers.

Pitohui dichrous

ADAPTATION

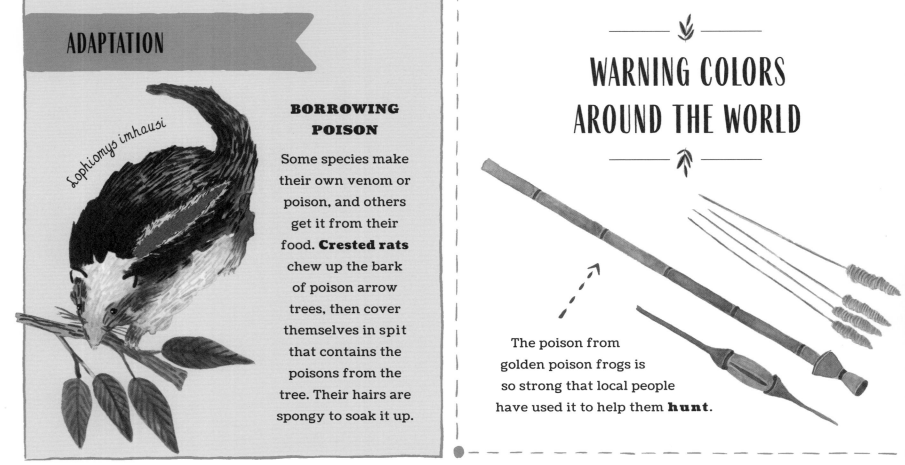

Lophiomys imhausi

BORROWING POISON

Some species make their own venom or poison, and others get it from their food. **Crested rats** chew up the bark of poison arrow trees, then cover themselves in spit that contains the poisons from the tree. Their hairs are spongy to soak it up.

WARNING COLORS AROUND THE WORLD

The poison from golden poison frogs is so strong that local people have used it to help them **hunt**.

Lophiomys imhausi

CRESTED RAT

These African rodents have black, white, and orange stripes, which warns predators that they are **poisonous**.

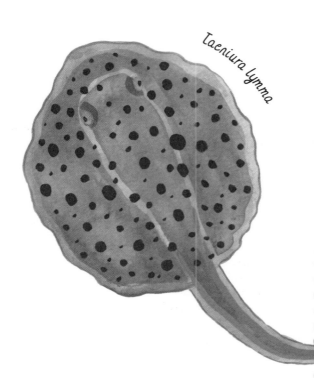
Taeniura lymma

EASTERN CORAL SNAKE

These snakes warn predators that they are **venomous** with black, yellow, and red stripes.

Micrurus fulvius

BLUESPOTTED RIBBONTAIL RAY

This stingray has bright blue spots and two spines on its long tail that can **inject venom**.

Emberá people from Colombia catch the frogs and simply rub **darts** over the frogs' skin.

Although there are many species called poison dart frogs, only **three** are used for making darts.

Their darts, now covered in deadly poison, are shot by **blowing** them through a pipe.

Phyllobates bicolor

Phyllobates aurotaenia

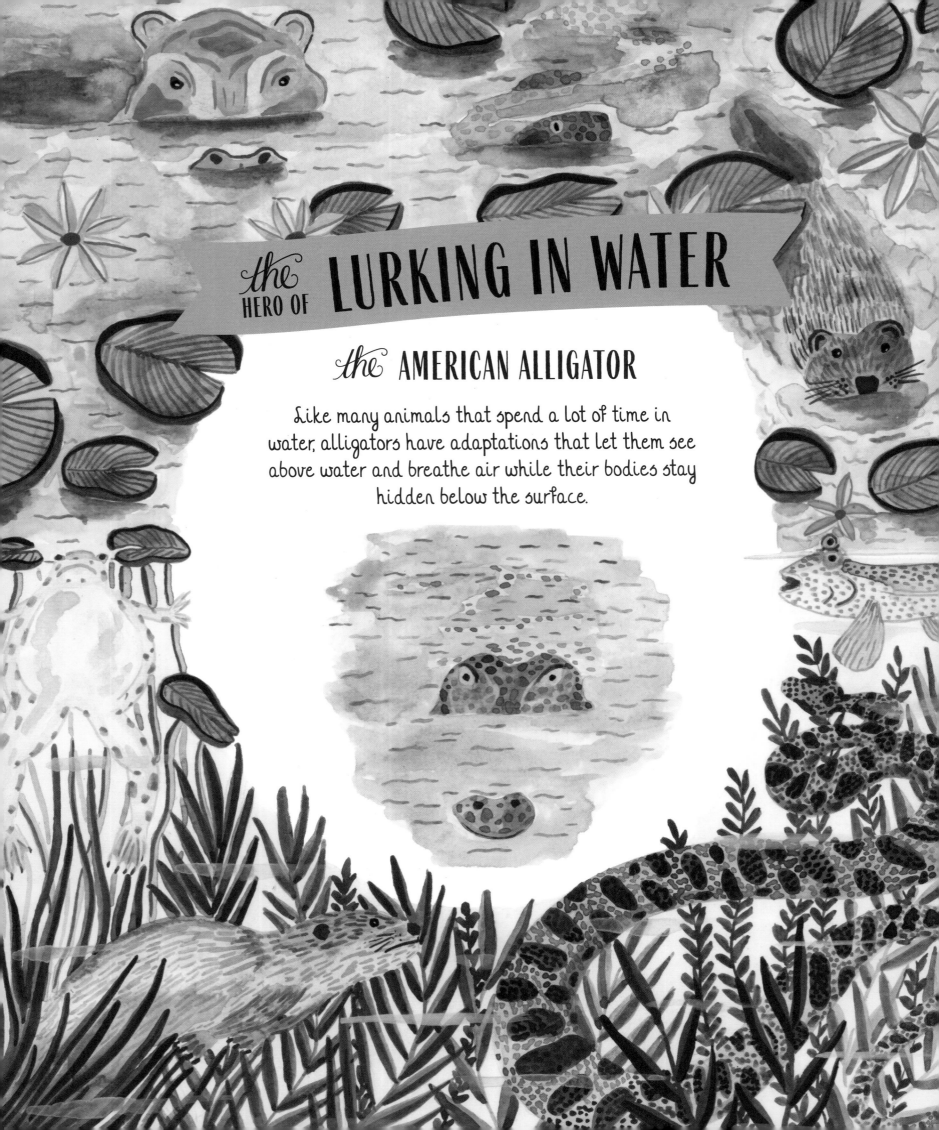

LURKING IN WATER
the HERO OF

the AMERICAN ALLIGATOR

Like many animals that spend a lot of time in water, alligators have adaptations that let them see above water and breathe air while their bodies stay hidden below the surface.

When humans swim, we have to work hard to get our mouths, noses, and eyes above water so we can breathe and see. To get around these problems, many swimming animals have eyes and noses at the very tops of their heads.

WHERE IN THE WILD?

American alligators live in swamps, lakes, and streams in the southeastern United States.

Although alligators and crocodiles usually like to be warm, some places where American alligators live get cold in winter. But even if the water starts to freeze, they stay below the surface with just their nose sticking out of the ice, so they can still breathe.

Alligator teeth are good for grabbing prey but not for chewing, so they swallow **stones** to help them grind up their food.

Their roar sounds like a **growling snore**. If they do this with their bodies just under the surface, the rumbling makes the water dance above them.

knobby backs look like ripples in the water.

raised nose and eyes

Alligators are **good mothers;** they build nests of warm, rotting plants to lay their eggs in and care for their young once they hatch.

A DANGEROUS DRINK

Alligator heads are quite flat, but their eyes and noses are raised up slightly, allowing them to see and breathe above the surface with their bodies hidden under the dark water. When an animal comes down to the water to drink, unaware that a huge predator is lurking, the alligator can leap out and grab them.

ALL ABOUT LURKING IN WATER

Mammals, reptiles, birds, and most amphibians need to breathe air. So if they spend time swimming—whether or not they need to sneak up on their prey or hide from predators—they have to hold part of their heads above water. Having their eyes and noses high on their heads makes life a lot easier.

GREEN ANACONDA

The world's largest snake lives in South American swamps and rivers. Like alligators, they hunt for birds, reptiles, and mammals with their bodies **underwater**.

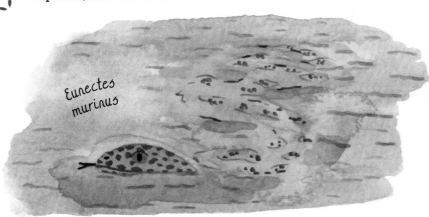

Eunectes murinus

HIPPOPOTAMUS

Hippos eat grass at **night** but spend most of their days in water, with their eyes, noses, and ears above the surface.

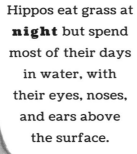

Hippopotamus amphibius

PACIFIC FOUR-EYED FISH

Although they don't breathe air, these fish hunt for insects at the **surface**. Each eye is split into two, with one half looking underwater and one half looking up.

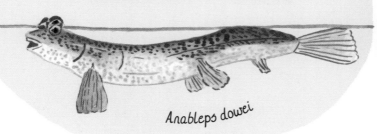

Anableps dowei

LURKING IN WATER AROUND THE WORLD

One Amazonian story explains that the **anaconda** was formed from a man and woman lying in a hammock when a great flood happened.

Chinese alligators may have been the origin of the dragon in Chinese culture.

EUROPEAN BEAVER

Beavers create lakes by building dams. Compared to other rodents, their noses and eyes are high on their heads as adaptations for **swimming**.

Castor fiber

AFRICAN CLAWED FROG

These amphibians often float with only their eyes and nostrils above water. They don't have tongues, so they just shovel food into their mouths with their **hands**.

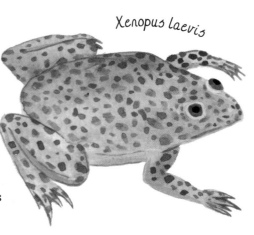

Xenopus laevis

NOSE POSITION

We can learn a lot about an animal's life from the features on its skull. Sharp teeth might tell us it eats meat, while massive eye-holes might mean they can see in the dark. If you ever spot a skull with its eyes and nose on top, it was probably a swimmer like the **American alligator**.

Alligator mississippiensis

According to a story from the Haida people of Canada, the first **beaver** was a woman who loved swimming, so she built dams to create a lake.

Taweret is an Ancient Egyptian goddess who was part **hippo**, part **crocodile**, and part **lion**. She protected mothers and babies.

the HERO OF HORNS & ANTLERS

the MOOSE

When animals need to protect themselves from harm or fight for mates or territory, they use weapons that have evolved to do just that. Impressive horns and antlers appear in many different groups.

Having weapons on your head makes sense, because you can put all your strength behind them. Many animals have horns, but only deer have antlers. Antlers are made of bone, have branches, and regrow every year. Moose are the largest living deer and have the largest antlers in the deer family.

huge, strong antlers

big lips and nose

WHERE IN THE WILD?

Moose live across the northern forests of Europe, Asia, and North America, where they feed on trees and shrubs.

In Europe, moose are called "elk," even though they are the same species, but the name "elk" is given to a different kind of deer in North America, which is a bit confusing!

Moose antlers are among the **largest** weapons of any animal, reaching more than 65 pounds (35 kg). That's like growing a ten-year-old child on your head every year.

Moose also use their antlers to **defend** against bears, wolves, tigers, and pumas, but these predators often hunt young moose, which don't have antlers.

ANNUAL ANTLERS

Male deer grow antlers every year for fighting over females during the breeding season. Once that's over, their antlers fall off and grow back the next year. Reindeer are the only species of deer where the females also have antlers—they use them to defend patches of food in winter.

Moose have a massive **noses** and **lips**. Their lips can grip food, and they can close their nostrils when feeding on underwater plants.

ALL ABOUT HORNS & ANTLERS

Life in the wild is tough—everything can become a battle, which is why many animals have evolved weapons. Unlike deer antlers, which are always made of bone and fall off each year, horns can be made of different materials and usually stay attached throughout an animal's life.

GREATER KUDU

Many antelope, including kudu, have massive horns to **fight** over mates. They have bone on the inside, covered with the same material that makes our hair and fingernails.

Tragelaphus strepsiceros

PRONGHORN

These American mammals have unusual horns, with permanent **bony centers**, like antelope horns, but with branched coatings that drop off and regrow each year.

Antilocapra americana

COAHUILACERATOPS

This Mexican dinosaur is related to the famous **Triceratops**, and it may have had the largest dino horns ever at more than 3 feet (1 m) long.

Coahuilaceratops magnacuerna

Rhinoplax vigil

HELMETED HORNBILL

These birds have solid ivory **"helmets"** on their heads, which they crash together in midair to fight over fruit trees.

Ceratotherium simum

WHITE RHINO

Rhino horns can reach about 3 feet (1 m) long but have no bone in them—they grow out of the **skin**, not the skull—and are used in defense against predators.

ADAPTATION

Cervus elaphus

LOCKING HORNS

Animals can hurt each other when fighting over mates or food, but their weapons are rarely used to kill. Most antlers and horns, like those of the **red deer** pictured, are shaped to lock together without causing serious injury.

Most competitions don't even involve a fight; once the animals have checked each other out, the one with the smallest weapons usually backs off.

HORNS & ANTLERS AROUND THE WORLD

Rhinos are among the first animals ever drawn by people—they appear in art around **30,000 years old** in Namibia and France.

The Hornbill Festival in India brings together all the tribes of Nagaland. It is named after the great **hornbill**.

Buceros bicornis

The word "moose" comes from the North American Algonquin language and means "**twig-eater**."

Many **headdresses** have been found in Yorkshire, England, and were carved over 10,000 years ago from red deer skulls with antlers. They may have been used as camouflage for hunting deer or as part of ritual costumes.

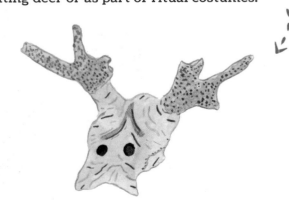

the HERO OF FISH-CATCHING SNOUTS

the COMMON DOLPHIN

Many predators rely on eating fish, and we can spot the same adaptations evolving in different groups of animals for snapping up these wriggly, often slimy animals without them being able to squirm away.

COMMON DOLPHIN
DELPHINUS DELPHIS

Dolphins have long, narrow snouts packed with simple, curved, pointy teeth. These are perfect for grabbing fast-moving fish from the water, and their teeth—shaped like slightly bent cones—lock together to make sure the fish can't escape their grip.

WHERE IN THE WILD?
Common dolphins are not very fussy about which kinds of small fish they eat.
They eat squid, so they can find a meal in lots of places. They live in large numbers in cool and tropical waters of the Atlantic, Pacific, and Indian oceans.

Common dolphins can dive to depths of more than 650 feet (200 m), but as they are mammals, they must return to the surface to **breathe**.

Because they're so simple, common dolphin teeth are good for **catching food** but not chewing it, so they swallow fish whole.

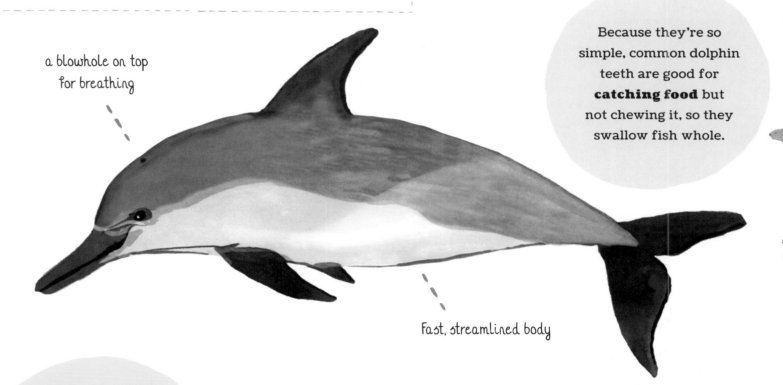

a blowhole on top for breathing

Fast, streamlined body

Common dolphins can have up to 240 teeth, which **fit tightly** together when their mouths close. Unlike most other mammals, all their teeth look the same.

FEEDING WITH FRIENDS
Common dolphins can be found in groups—called pods—with hundreds or even thousands of individuals. They can work together to make hunting easier by herding the fish into tightly packed balls—or pushing large numbers of fish up against the surface and then taking turns swimming and grabbing a mouthful.

ALL ABOUT FISH-CATCHING SNOUTS

Fish are easy food to find and high in energy, so the same adaptations we see in dolphins for catching fish have evolved in other groups of animals across millions of years. If animals live around water and have narrow snouts with simple, grabbing teeth, there's a good chance they catch fish.

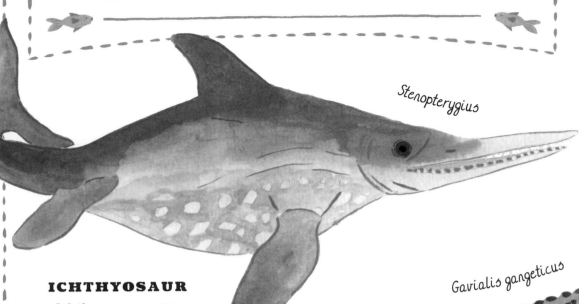

Stenopterygius

Gavialis gangeticus

ICHTHYOSAUR

Ichthyosaurs were **extinct**, swimming, fish-eating reptiles from the time of the dinosaurs, but they looked almost exactly like dolphins.

GHARIAL

These massive, narrow-snouted, **endangered** relatives of crocodiles feed on fish in Indian, Nepalese, and Bangladeshi rivers.

ADAPTATION

Gavialis gangeticus

FAST FACES

The teeth of fish catchers fit together closely to hold on tightly to their prey, but one reason that their snouts are so slim is that thin shapes are easy to move through the water, so their narrow snouts allow them to **strike** quickly to capture fish.

FISH-CATCHING SNOUTS AROUND THE WORLD

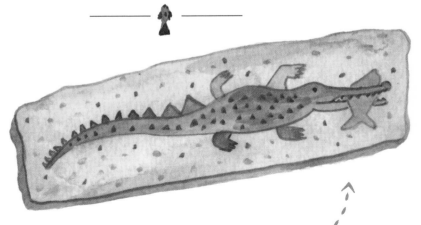

Gharials have been important to the people who live alongside them since ancient times.

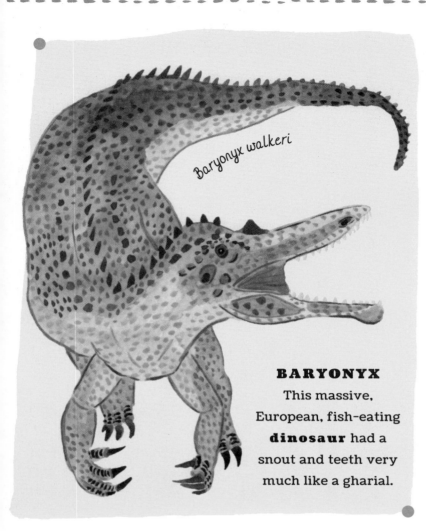

Baryonyx walkeri

LONGNOSE GAR

The long, thin jaws of this North American fish—packed with teeth—are perfectly evolved for **snatching** other fish.

Lepisosteus osseus

Mergus serrator

BARYONYX

This massive, European, fish-eating **dinosaur** had a snout and teeth very much like a gharial.

RED-BREASTED MERGANSER

Birds don't have teeth, but these ducks have evolved **saw-like edges** on their narrow beaks to help them grip fish.

Clay gharials were made in the Indus Valley city of **Mohenjo-daro** more than 4,000 years ago.

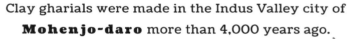

Gharials are named after a pot called a **"ghara"** in Hindi, as male gharials have a pot-shaped lump around their nose for attracting mates.

Gharials have been killed for these lumps due to local beliefs in their mystical powers, but it is mainly **habitat loss** that has made them endangered.

the HERO OF ECHOLOCATION

the COMMON PIPISTRELLE BAT

Some animals that are active in the dark sense the world by making sounds, then listening for the tiny echoes the sounds make as they bounce off everything around them.

COMMON PIPISTRELLE BAT
PIPISTRELLUS PIPISTRELLUS

Bats are the masters of echolocation: the power of finding their way, or finding other animals, by bouncing sound off their surroundings. It's also done by some other animals that come out at night, or spend time deep in caves or underwater where there is little light.

WHERE IN THE WILD?
Although they are tiny, pipistrelles are among the easiest bats to spot.

Found in most of Europe and parts of Asia and North Africa, they often sleep in buildings and hunt around streetlamps, catching insects that fly around the lights. They can be found in many other habitats too, including woodlands and wetlands.

A pipistrelle can weigh less than a sheet of **paper**—they're more than 300 times lighter than the biggest bats.

forward-facing thumbs helpful for climbing

wings formed by stretched skin

To get the clearest picture of where the insect is when they are getting close to their prey, bats can make up to **200 calls** per second.

Most adult humans can't hear bat calls, but children's ears may be able to detect the high-pitched **clicks** they make as they hunt.

A FACE FOR HEARING
Echolocating bats make super-high-pitched calls and listen for their echoes with their massive ears as they fly, allowing them to sense objects around them and find prey at high speeds. Some bats, like horseshoe bats, call through their noses, which are folded into strange shapes to help them aim the sounds in a specific direction.

ALL ABOUT ECHOLOCATION

Bats flying fast and hunting insects in complete darkness without hitting anything is perhaps the most impressive use of echolocation, but other groups of animals have evolved this superpower for use in completely different habitats, from the dark, deep ocean to the gloomy forest floor.

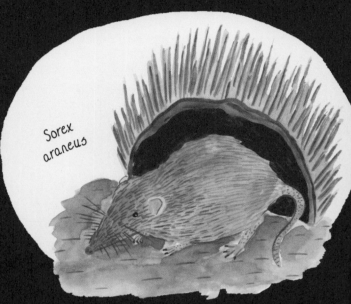

Steatornis caripensis

OILBIRD
Echolocation is very rare in birds, but this South American species uses it to fly through the **dark caves** where they nest.

SPERM WHALE
Whales and dolphins use echolocation to find food in the vast ocean. Sperm whales produce the **loudest sounds** of any animal on Earth with their noses.

Sorex araneus

COMMON SHREW
These tiny, squeaky mammals use echolocation to **move** safely around rocks and plants on the ground, and also in dark tunnels

Physeter macrocephalus

ECHOLOCATION AROUND THE WORLD

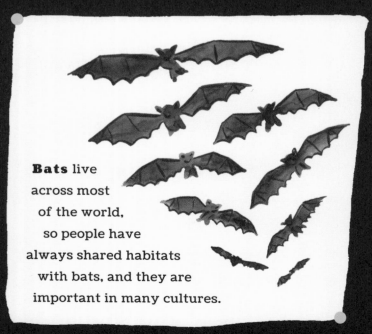

Bats live across most of the world, so people have always shared habitats with bats, and they are important in many cultures.

Bats help farmers by catching **insects** that can damage crops. Farmers can build bat nest-boxes so that more of them live nearby.

VIETNAMESE PYGMY DORMOUSE

These little rodents are almost **blind** but can still climb around trees by making calls and listening for how they echo.

Typhlomys cinereus chapensis

LOWLAND STREAKED TENREC

These spiny Madagascan mammals **click** their tongues to use echolocation to find their way around the rainforest at night.

Hemicentetes semispinosus

ESCAPING ECHOES

Bats hunt their prey using echolocation, but some insects have evolved a way of tricking them. African moon moths have large wings with long, streaming tails that flutter as they fly. This changes the way that the bat's calls bounce off them, confusing the bat so they can't find the moth.

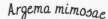

Argema mimosae

Bats were among the animals drawn on rock walls by some of the first people to reach South America, around **13,000 years** ago. Their paintings survive today.

Bats are lucky in China and are often found in art. The Chinese word for bat—**"Fu"**— sounds the same as the word for good fortune.

the HERO OF COUNTERSHADING

the GENTOO PENGUIN

Animals often use camouflage to hide against their background. But what if their backgrounds are completely different when you look at them from above and below? Countershading colors can solve this.

GENTOO PENGUIN
PYGOSCELIS PAPUA

In the sea, many species have dark backs and white bellies. This countershading means that if you are above them, their backs are camouflaged against the dark, deep ocean below; but if you are below them, their light bellies match the color of the bright sky above.

WHERE IN THE WILD?

Gentoo penguins hunt in the seas around Antarctica, Chile, and Argentina, where they catch fish, squid, and shrimp in shallow water near the coasts.

Large populations come to nest among the grass or stony beaches of the Falkland Islands, South Georgia, and the Antarctic Peninsula.

Penguins can't fly in the air, but they do have strong wing muscles: They **flap** their wings when they swim and "fly" underwater.

view from above

Gentoo penguins make nests out of rocks and give **rocks** as gifts to their mates. But sometimes they sneak up and steal these rocks from other nests.

view from below

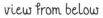

There are 18 different species of penguin, but they all have **black backs** and **white bellies**. Gentoos are one of the biggest.

NOW YOU SEE ME, NOW YOU DON'T

Out of the water, adult penguins are quite safe from predators, so they don't need to hide— it doesn't matter if their black backs stand out against the snow. But they do need camouflage in the **sea** to avoid the huge seals that hunt them and so their own prey don't spot them.

ALL ABOUT COUNTERSHADING

When you're underwater, predators and prey can come from above or below you. Countershading is such a powerful adaptation for hiding in the water that many swimming animals have evolved a dark back and a light belly. But it works on land too, as it helps hide animals' shadows.

GREAT AUK
These birds evolved to do what penguins do, but lived in the **North Atlantic**. They looked and behaved just like penguins, but were not closely related to them. They were hunted to extinction in the 1840s.

Pinguinus impennis

ORCA (KILLER WHALE)
Orcas don't have any natural predators, but they use countershading to **hide** from their prey.

Orcinus orca

UPSIDE-DOWN CATFISH
The colors on this African fish are opposite: they have darker bellies and lighter backs. This is because they feed belly-up at the **surface**.

Synodontis batensoda

LOVELY HATCHETFISH
In deep water, predators look for the dark shapes of prey against the dim light from above, but hatchetfish produce their **own light** from their bellies as camouflage.

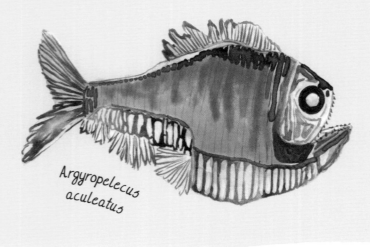

Argyropelecus aculeatus

GRANT'S GAZELLE
Countershading doesn't just work in water—it helps on **land** too. Like many land mammals, these antelope have darker backs and lighter belles.

Nanger granti

COUNTERSHADING AROUND THE WORLD

In Australia, Thaua people and orcas teamed up to **hunt** whales. The orcas would chase a whale into a bay, where the people would catch it, and share the meat with the orcas.

A grave of someone who died 4,000 years ago in **Newfoundland**, Canada, contains more than 150 great auk beaks—it is thought they were attached to the person's cloak.

The blackbuck antelope, which has obvious countershading, is said to pull the chariot of the Hindu moon god **Chandra**.

The word "penguin" was originally a name for great auks. It may come from the Welsh for "white head": pen gwyn.

ADAPTATION

Vulpes vulpes

HIDING SHADOWS

Good camouflage hides you against your background, but bright sunlight can make the upper parts of animals shine and creates obvious shadows on their bellies. Countershading cancels this out: From deer and squirrels to **red foxes** and tigers, the parts that face upward are dark to reduce their shine, and the lower parts are light to reduce the shadows.

ANT-EATING SNOUTS

the GIANT ANTEATER

One ant isn't much of a meal, but where you find one, you often find millions more. Animals that have evolved ways of catching mouthfuls of ants—like long, sticky tongues and tube-shaped faces—can always find a meal.

GIANT ANTEATER
MYRMECOPHAGA TRIDACTYLA

Ants and termites are small insects that live across the world, often building large nests that contain huge numbers inside their colony. Species like anteaters have evolved to feast on them, gobbling up adults, eggs, and larvae with their perfectly adapted snouts.

WHERE IN THE WILD?

Giant anteaters, along with their relatives the silky anteaters and tamanduas, live in South and Central America.

Because ants and termites live in lots of different habitats, so do giant anteaters, including rainforests, swamps, woodlands, and grasslands.

Their **tongues** can stick nearly 2 feet (0.6 m) out of their mouths, flicking 150 times each minute. They can quickly swallow thousands of insects.

Anteater **snouts** are very long, but their mouths are very small—found right at the tip. They also don't have any teeth.

strong, hairy tail

long, sticky tongue

termites

Anteaters have huge, **bushy tails**, which they sleep under like a blanket and use for support when they stand up to fight predators.

ANTS FIGHT BACK

Many ants bite and have stings in their tails, or spray nasty chemicals; some species have "soldiers" that defend their nests with larger jaws and more powerful stings. Their thick skin and hair help protect them. Anteaters must work fast at each nest before the soldier ants rush out.

ALL ABOUT ANT-EATING SNOUTS

Ants are found on every continent (except Antarctica), and animals around the world have evolved to eat them. The same adaptations can be found in many of these animals: long snouts to reach into the nest and collect insects with wriggly, sticky tongues, and either simple teeth or none at all.

AARDVARK

This African species is the world's largest burrowing mammal. Their **big ears** help them listen for predators while they're busy licking up ants.

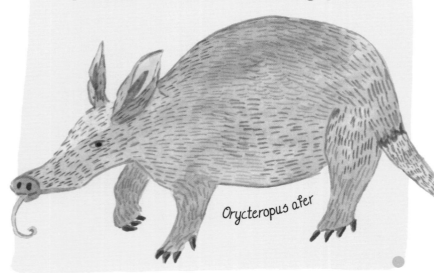

Orycteropus afer

Tachyglossus aculeatus

SHORT-BEAKED ECHIDNA

Because their snouts are so similar, scientists once thought Australian echidnas were closely related to anteaters, but they're actually related to the **platypus**.

ADAPTATION

AWESOME CLAWS

Ants and termites can build massive nests out of wood or with hard mud and spit, and lots of ant-eating animals have impressive claws and strong arms for digging into these nests to get their meals. **Giant anteater** claws are so long that they have to walk on their knuckles to keep their claws off the ground.

Myrmecophaga tridactyla

ANT-EATING SNOUTS AROUND THE WORLD

Stories from Brazil say that giant anteaters are **bad luck** if one crosses your path.

Manis pentadactyla

CHINESE PANGOLIN

Pangolins are scaly mammals from Asia and Africa, with **tongues** that are almost the same length as their bodies.

Myrmecobius fasciatus

Colaptes auratus

NORTHERN FLICKER

These North American birds are members of the **woodpecker** family, but rather than pecking wood, they pluck ants and other insects from the grass.

NUMBAT

Numbats are marsupials from Australia. Their long, sticky tongues can catch up to **20,000 termites** every day.

Echidnas have appeared in **art** across Australia for many thousands of years, including drawings that are carved deep into solid rock.

In different parts of Africa, pangolins are thought to bring good fortune, while harming one can bring bad luck.

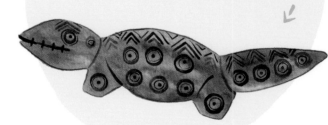

Aardvark means **"earth pig"** in Afrikaans because they are such good diggers and the end of their nose looks like a pig's.

the HERO OF PADDLING FEET

the PLATYPUS

Webs between toes are excellent adaptations that allow animals to turn their feet into paddles. These big, flat feet push hard against the water, making these animals strong swimmers.

PLATYPUS
ORNITHORHYNCHUS ANATINUS

Many animals must walk on land and swim in water, and they need feet that let them do both. Platypuses are the masters of this. They have large webs of skin on their hands that stretch out beyond their long claws.

WHERE IN THE WILD?
Platypuses need to hunt in water, so these mammals can't live in the drier parts of Australia.
Instead, they are found across Victoria and the eastern edge of the country and on the island of Tasmania. This means they can survive the hot tropical forests of the north as well as the freezing mountain lakes of the south.

They don't have any teeth. Instead, they have horny ridges in their bills to grind up their food.

Although they are only about 16 inches (40 cm) long, female platypuses can dig burrows more than 30 feet (9 m) long to make their nests, where they lay their eggs.

bill that detects electricity.

feet for swimming, walking, and digging

Platypuses catch worms, crayfish, and insects underwater with their eyes and ears closed—they can detect the electricity given off by their prey's muscles.

DIFFERENT FEET FOR DIFFERENT FEATS
Platypuses swim with their webbed front feet. Their back feet are used for other jobs: They can reach all over their body to groom their thick fur, which is important for keeping warm in cold water; and when they dig their burrows, their back feet lock into the soil so they can push hard with their front feet.

ALL ABOUT PADDLING FEET

Webbed feet are so helpful for swimming that many birds, mammals, amphibians, and reptiles have evolved to have them. But big webbed feet can make walking difficult. Species that spend more time in water often have feet that are more paddle-shaped than those that walk a lot.

EUROPEAN COMMON FROG

These amphibians have extra-long toes at the end of their powerful legs, making their webbed feet even bigger.

Rana temporaria

CALIFORNIA SEA LION

Unlike seals, which swim with their back feet, sea lions swim mainly using their huge webbed front flippers.

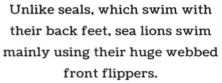

Zalophus californianus

TUFTED DUCK

These ducks' legs are very far back on their bodies, which helps them dive underwater for food, but it gives them poor balance when waddling on land.

Aythya fuligula

GREAT CRESTED GREBE

Instead of joined-up webs, these water birds just have extra flaps of skin around each toe to help them paddle.

Podiceps cristatus

LOGGERHEAD SEA TURTLE

Sea turtles only come onto land to lay eggs. Their hands and feet have evolved into long paddles, which are great for swimming, but make walking difficult.

Caretta caretta

TRANSFORMER FEET

Platypus feet are amazing—they have tools for different parts of their lives. In water, their webs fold out to make huge swimming paddles. On land, they protect their soft webs by tucking them into their fists, and walk on their knuckles. And when they build their long burrows, the webs fold back to reveal long digging claws.

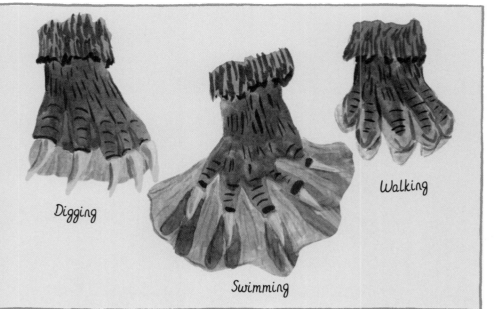

Digging

Swimming

Walking

PADDLING FEET AROUND THE WORLD

In Hindu and some Native American stories, the world is carried on a giant turtle's back, and Chinese mythology says turtle legs hold up the sky.

SAN FRANCISCO

You don't normally see massive mammals in the middle of a city, but California sea lions hang out among the tourists by the piers in San Francisco.

The lamia is a mythical creature from the Basque Country of Spain and France with the body of a beautiful woman but the feet of a duck.

the HERO OF **WOOD-PECKING**

the AYE-AYE

Many insects live inside wood, building tunnels that keep them safe from most predators, but not all succeed in hiding: Some birds and mammals have evolved impressive adaptations to get hold of these hidden insects.

AYE-AYE
DAUBENTONIA MADAGASCARIENSIS

Three tricks are needed to catch insects in their woody homes: hearing where exactly they are hiding, pecking holes in solid trees, and pulling the prey out of their tunnels. Aye-ayes are primates that have adaptations to do all three.

WHERE IN THE WILD?

Aye-ayes are an endangered lemur that come out at night to feed on insects, fruit, and seeds in Madagascar.

Madagascar is a huge island to the east of the African continent. It is home to more than 100 species of lemurs, which are a group of primates related to monkeys.

Aye-ayes use their large front teeth, which curve forward and never stop growing, to cut into the wood to reach the insects' burrows.

big ears for hearing hiding insects

An aye-aye's middle finger is extremely long and skinny—perfectly shaped to hook its prey out of their narrow tunnels.

long, skinny middle fingers

Aye-ayes find insects by tapping on wood and listening for hollow spaces inside. They have huge ears to help them hear.

NOSE-PECKING?

The adaptations that help aye-ayes hunt insects inside wood are handy for other jobs too. Their strong front teeth help them crack into their favorite nuts, and scientists recently discovered that they can use their extra-long finger to pick their noses, reaching deep inside and eating the snot. (Don't try this at home!)

ALL ABOUT WOOD-PECKING

Woodpeckers are a large group of birds found throughout much of the world that have perfectly evolved to catch insect larvae hiding in wood. However, in countries without woodpeckers–like Madagascar, Australia, and New Zealand– other animals have evolved to do the same thing.

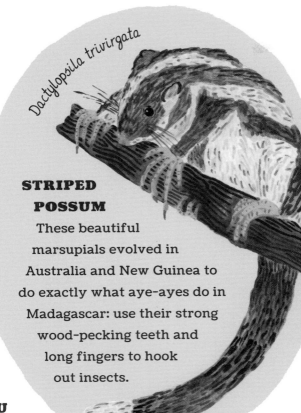

Dactylopsila trivirgata

STRIPED POSSUM

These beautiful marsupials evolved in Australia and New Guinea to do exactly what aye-ayes do in Madagascar: use their strong wood-pecking teeth and long fingers to hook out insects.

GREAT SPOTTED WOODPECKER

Woodpeckers have a special skull and beak that can survive being hammered against a tree to get to insects. Their sticky tongues are so long that they wrap around their brains when not extended.

Dendrocopos major

'AKIAPŌLĀ'AU

These Hawaiian birds use their strong lower bill to tap and peck into wood, then their narrow, curved upper bill to hook out the insects.

Hemignathus wilsoni

WOOD-PECKING AROUND THE WORLD

Aye-ayes are involved in many different beliefs in Madagascar, probably because they look unusual, with orange eyes, giant ears, a single skinny finger on each hand, and scraggly hair.

Some people think that seeing an aye-aye is a sign that terrible things will happen.

WOODPECKER FINCH

The tongue of this small bird from the Galápagos Islands is too short to catch insects in wood. Instead, it has evolved to use sticks to pull out its prey.

Camarhynchus pallidus

HUIA

The males of these extinct New Zealand birds had a bill like an axe for digging insects out of wood; and the females had thin, curved bills to pluck them out of their tunnels.

Heteralocha acutirostris

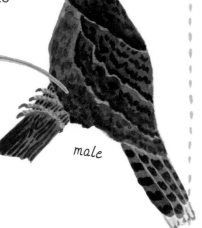

female

male

HAMMER HEADS

You might think that when a woodpecker, such as the **pileated woodpecker** pictured, hammers a tree with its head, it might hurt its brain, but their skulls are specially adapted to prevent this. The bone is strong but slightly spongy to act as a cushion, and the muscles and joints send most of the power through the body instead of the brain.

Dryocopus pileatus

But not everyone feels this way: In some Madagascan villages, people **protect aye-ayes** because they eat the insects that damage the food people grow.

The huia is sacred in **Māori** culture, and the white-tipped, black feathers were worn by people of importance.

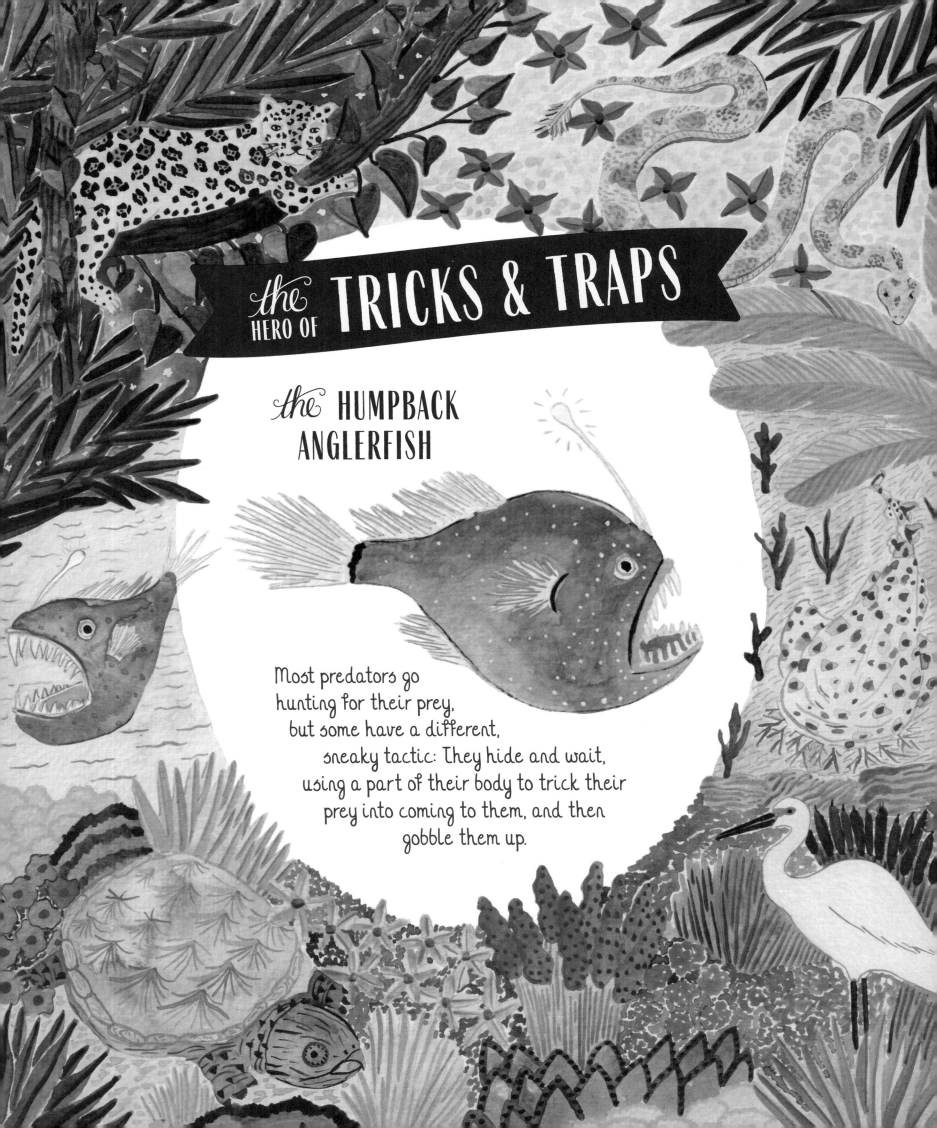

the HERO OF TRICKS & TRAPS

the HUMPBACK ANGLERFISH

Most predators go
hunting for their prey,
but some have a different,
sneaky tactic: They hide and wait,
using a part of their body to trick their
prey into coming to them, and then
gobble them up.

HUMPBACK ANGLERFISH
MELANOCETUS JOHNSONII

When people go fishing, they use bait to attract the fish. Some animals do the same thing, but they have turned part of their own body into the bait, called a "lure." Anglerfish lures are a little "fishing rod" on their heads.

WHERE IN THE WILD?
Humpback anglerfish, also called blackdevils, live deep in the world's oceans—over a mile (1.6 km) below the surface.

It's dark down there, and at that depth there isn't much to eat. Most deep-sea fish need special tricks to find their food, but anglerfish make sure their food finds them.

There is a thin rod on the snout of these anglerfish with a little bag at the end of it full of bacteria that make their own light.

a glowing "fishing rod"

In the darkness, other animals are attracted toward this light; It acts as bait to bring them close, then the anglerfish eats them.

a stretchy stomach

Anglerfish have enormous mouths packed with long teeth, and their stomachs are so stretchy that they can swallow fish that are even bigger than them.

FEMALE FISHING FISH
In some anglerfish, only the females have a fishing rod, and they are many times larger than the males. Finding mates in the deep, dark ocean is difficult, so in some species, when a pair do find each other, the male permanently attaches to the female, so she does all the hunting to feed them both.

ALL ABOUT TRICKS & TRAPS

Anglerfish aren't the only animals that trick their prey into coming near before grabbing them. There are other species that have evolved incredible lures to attract their meals—particularly fish—into getting dangerously close. They use their own bodies as bait. Some of their lures look surprisingly like food.

SPIDER-TAILED VIPER

This snake eats birds that are tricked into thinking the snake's tail is a spider—it even has a fake spider body and legs.

Pseudocerastes urarachnoides

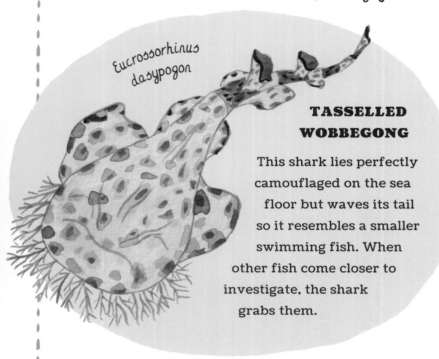

Eucrossorhinus dasypogon

TASSELLED WOBBEGONG

This shark lies perfectly camouflaged on the sea floor but waves its tail so it resembles a smaller swimming fish. When other fish come closer to investigate, the shark grabs them.

SNOWY EGRET

These birds stand in shallow water and flick their tongue on the surface. Fish think it's food and come to take the bait—but instead, the egret eats them.

Egretta thula

JAGUAR

These big cats fish with their tails—they move them gently on the water, and prey are attracted to the movement before being eaten.

Panthera onca

ALLIGATOR SNAPPING TURTLE

These reptiles' tongues look just like worms. They open their mouths and wiggle their tongues, waiting for a fish to swim in to grab it, then they snap their jaws shut.

Macrochelys temminckii

ADAPTATION

TRAP SETTING

For these traps to work, these animals must make sure their prey are attracted to the bait but can't see the rest of their body. **Alligator snapping turtles** are masters of disguise. Although they are huge (some weighing more than an adult human), their muddy colors and bumpy shells allow them to lie hidden underwater.

TRICKS & TRAPS AROUND THE WORLD

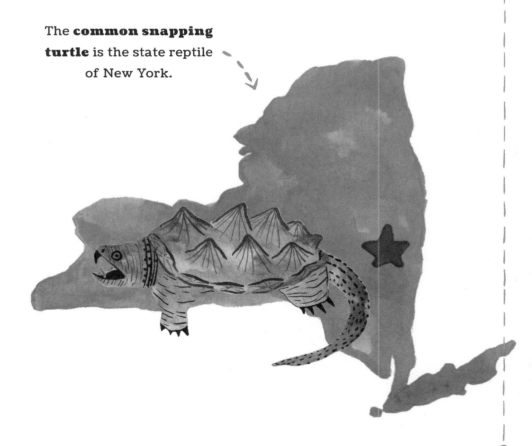

Monkfish are a kind of anglerfish that are often caught to be sold as food. Unfortunately, the way they are caught damages their habitat on the sea floor.

The **common snapping turtle** is the state reptile of New York.

Egrets are symbols of peace for many Native American tribes, and act as wise elders in some traditional stories.

the HERO OF ANIMAL ARMOR

the TREE PANGOLIN

When in danger, some animals hide, some run, some use poison or venom, and some have weapons. Others have evolved to protect their soft parts from predators' teeth and claws by using armor.

TREE PANGOLIN
PHATAGINUS TRICUSPIS

Your skin is amazing—it is waterproof, it can keep you warm or cool you down, and it can heal itself. It's quite tough, but it is not hard . . . unlike pangolin skin. Pangolins have evolved to be the world's only scaly mammals.

WHERE IN THE WILD?

Tree pangolins are good climbers, and they feed on ants and termites in the forests of West and Central Africa.

Three other species of pangolin also live in Africa, and four more live in Asia. Sadly, they are all threatened with extinction—their armor does not protect them against people.

Tree pangolins' big claws don't just help them break open insect nests but are also handy for climbing trees.

Pangolin scales grow out of their skin and are made of the same material as our hair and fingernails—a protein called "keratin."

strong claws for climbing

ROLL UP, ROLL UP

Large scales cover tree pangolins' bodies except parts of their face, their bellies, and the insides of their legs. If they feel scared, they roll up into a ball to protect these soft parts, and mothers curl around their babies to keep them safe too. Normally, youngsters ride on their mother's long tail.

a tail that is like an extra hand

Their long tail is also an adaptation for climbing: They can use it like a fifth leg to grip branches.

ALL ABOUT ARMOR

Insects have a hard skeleton on the outside of their bodies and no bones on the inside. Vertebrates have their bony skeleton on the insides of their bodies, and most have soft coverings, but in some groups, they've evolved a hard coating too. This armor can be made from different materials.

BRAZILIAN THREE-BANDED ARMADILLO

When this armored mammal curls up, its triangular head and tail fit together tightly to make a perfect ball.

Tolypeutes tricinctus

Terrapene carolina carolina

EASTERN BOX TURTLE

This American reptile has a hinge in its shell. When it pulls its head and legs inside, it can close up like a box.

ADAPTATION

SKIN WITH BONE

We know that skin can be soft, slimy, scaly, feathered, or furry, but did you know that it can also be bony? Animals like **nine-banded armadillos**, crocodiles, and some dinosaurs grow lumps of bone within their skin. These bones are called "osteoderms" (meaning "bone-skin") and show that bones are not always on the inside.

Dasypus novemcinctus

ARMOR AROUND THE WORLD

In Venda, Zulu, and some other **African cultures**, pangolins are believed to come down from the sky during heavy rain.

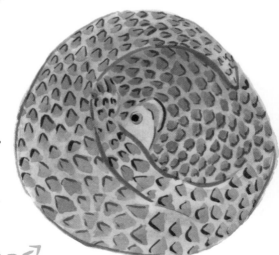

ANKYLOSAUR

You don't have to be small for armor to be helpful—these huge, plant-eating dinosaurs had sheets of bone in their skin to protect them from predators.

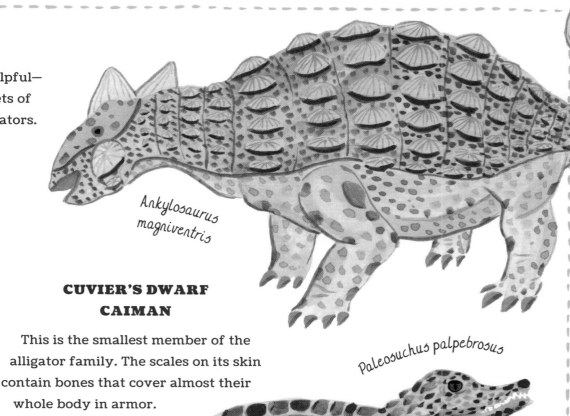

Ankylosaurus magniventris

THORNBACK COWFISH

These fish have hard, armored scales arranged in hexagonal shapes, making their bodies into solid boxes. Because of this, they can't swim fast.

Lactoria fornasini

CUVIER'S DWARF CAIMAN

This is the smallest member of the alligator family. The scales on its skin contain bones that cover almost their whole body in armor.

Paleosuchus palpebrosus

The word for armadillo in the Aztec language **Nahuatl** is ayotochtli, which means "turtle rabbit," as they have a head like a rabbit and a shell like a turtle.

In **Brazil**, caiman teeth are believed to protect people against snake-bites, and their skulls are sometimes placed outside houses to scare away spirits.

Pangolins are at risk of **extinction** because people hunt them for their scales for use in traditional Asian medicine.

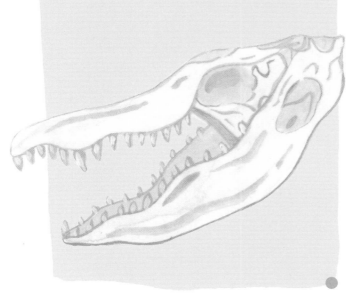

GLOSSARY

ADAPTATION – something an animal species has evolved to suit where and how it lives

AMPHIBIANS – a group of damp-skinned vertebrates that spend time on land and in water. They produce eggs without shells.

BIRDS – a group of vertebrates with feathers, most of which can fly

CAMOUFLAGE – an adaptation that helps animals blend into their environments, usually through their coloring or shape

CONVERGENT EVOLUTION – when the same adaptations evolve separately in different groups

GLIDING – flying without flapping wings

LARVA – the young stage of some animals, in which they appear very different from their adult form

LURE – something that attracts an animal to come closer, like a bait

MAMMALS – warm-blooded vertebrates that feed their young with milk and usually have fur

MARSUPIALS – mammals that produce tiny babies, which they mostly carry in a pouch

NOCTURNAL – animals that are mainly active at night

POISON – toxic chemicals that are harmful when eaten or drunk

PREDATOR – meat-eaters that hunt other animals

PREY – animals that are hunted by predators

REPTILES – animals with scaly skin, most of which are cold-blooded and lay eggs

TERRITORY – an animal's home area, which they work hard to defend

VENOM – toxic chemicals that are harmful when injected into a victim

VERTEBRATE – animals with backbones: fish, amphibians, birds, reptiles, and mammals

WEBBED FEET – feet with a membrane or tissue that connects or surrounds the toes to help with swimming

FURTHER READING

Links to online resources to learn more:

Animal Diversity Web – animaldiversity.org

Mongabay Kids – kids.mongabay.com

Defenders of Wildlife – defenders.org

International Union for Conservation of Nature – iucn.org

National Geographic – natgeokids.com

World Wildlife Fund – worldwildlife.org

For my niece—and editor—Sadie Newman
—J.A.

To my two wild animals, Jaiah and Francis!
—S.B.M.

The illustrations in this book were created in watercolor and gouache paints. Set in A Thousand Years, Coustard, Farmhouse, Haute, and Moonflower.

Library of Congress Control Number 2024947625
ISBN 978-1-4197-7699-1

Text © 2025 Jack Ashby
Illustrations © 2025 Sara Boccaccini Meadows
Book design by Nicola Price and Maisy Ruffels
Cover © Magic Cat 2025

First published in the United Kingdom in 2025 by Magic Cat Publishing Ltd. First published in North America in 2025 by Magic Cat Publishing, an imprint of ABRAMS. All rights reserved. No portion of this book may be reproduced, stored in a retrieval system, or transmitted in any form or by any means, mechanical, electronic, photocopying, recording, or otherwise, without written permission from the publisher.

Printed and bound in China
10 9 8 7 6 5 4 3 2 1

Abrams books are available at special discounts when purchased in quantity for premiums and promotions as well as fundraising or educational use. Special editions can also be created to specification. For details, contact specialsales@abramsbooks.com or the address below.

ABRAMS The Art of Books
195 Broadway, New York, NY 10007
abramsbooks.com